Praise for Bear

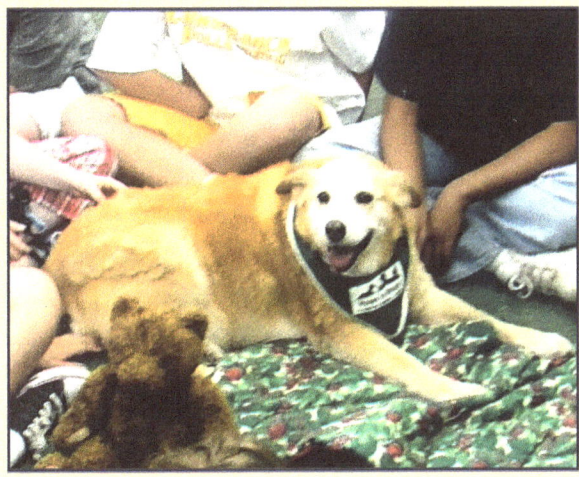

"Bear became a classmate to the students. She attended field trips, volunteer breakfasts, Special Olympics, and holidays with the class. I cannot thank you enough for the impact that you and Bear have had on the lives in my classroom. What wonderful times we have had!"

Carol Sharp, teacher, Lifeskills

"Bear was special, and really nice. Sometimes I have a hard time with my feelings, but when Bear was here, I feel good."

Lifeskills student

"Bear is patient when I read, and she's very fuzzy."

Lifeskills student

"Thank you Bear for helping me learn to read."

Lifeskills student

"Bear, reading to you makes me feel great. Thank you for taking time out of your busy schedule to come and visit with me. I love you; you are my best friend."

Lifeskills student

"What Bear did for me was she listened to me read my report. She made me feel really, really good."

Lifeskills student

"Bear, thank you for coming to visit me. It makes me feel happy and cheerful when you visit."

Lifeskills student

"Congratulations to Bear and you as Honorable Mentions for the Beyond Limits Therapy Animal Awards. The recognition is well deserved."

Lawrence J. Novell, Past President, CEO Delta Society (now Pet Partners)

Bear
a true story

An inspirational book celebrating the deep bond between humans and animals and the joys and healing power of unconditional love.

Windswept Books
Oregon USA
www.windsweptbooks.com

Copyright 2024 by Susanne Severeid
All Rights Reserved.

The book author retains sole copyright to her contributions to this book. No part of this book may be used or reproduced by any means without the written permission of the author except in the case of brief quotations embodied in critical articles and reviews.

With special thanks to Tyler, Jaclyn, and Deven for permission to use their wonderful illustrations.

All photos copyright by Susanne Severeid unless otherwise credited.
Author photo: copyright Pablo van Renterghem
www.pablovanphotography.com
Thanks to Beatrice Jacobs for her creative input and encouragement along the way.

Book design: Maggie McLaughlin
Thanks to John Cronin for his help with proofreading.

And special thanks to Tony and Pablo for their love and help.

Library of Congress Control Number: Applied for
ISBN: 978-0-9909528-4-8

First Edition

Printed in the United States of America

*This book is dedicated to all of Bear's students
who have given us so very much and
to their wonderful, hardworking,
and caring teachers.*

And, of course, to Bear herself.

*With special thanks to the volunteers
who give so generously of their time to make these
valuable community programs work.*

*For more information about such programs,
visit www.petpartners.org*

About the Program: "The Benefits of Reading to Pets: Children who are learning to read are often hesitant about their reading abilities. Many kids feel more at ease reading to pets, who are simply there to listen—not to judge how well they are reading."

Courtesy Pet Partners (www.petpartners.org)

A special note to you from Bear

Thank you for buying this book. You are helping children become better readers and helping homeless animals find new and loving homes because a portion of the sale of this book will be donated to these programs. Please remember to spay and neuter your pets to reduce the number of animals who end up in shelters each year. And if you do get a pet, always take good care of it. Remember, we need lots of love!

Please also consider adopting an older pet, like me. After all, we're not really "old"—we're just more experienced. And think of all the advantages: we're housebroken and don't chew up everything in sight!

Thanks, and a **big** bear hug from me,

Bear

Lost

The first time I saw Bear, she was behind bars.

Not because she had done anything wrong, but because she was in our local animal shelter.

She had been found wandering around in the woods near Flagstaff without a nametag or microchip. And, so far, no one had come by to claim her and take her home.

She looked so sad.

I looked at the card stuck on the door of her metal cage. All it said was, "Big yellow dog. Lab/Retriever Mix. 10 years old."

Ten years old? That's pretty old for a dog, I thought. But a dog of any age can give just as much love…and still needs a home just as badly.

I walked on, but I couldn't stop thinking about that big, yellow dog.

I thought about her as I drove home. I thought about her as I ate dinner. I even dreamt about her. I don't know why. But I did.

A few days later, I went back to the shelter to help a friend. She rescues dogs, and there were two dogs that she had found homes for, but not for the big, yellow dog.

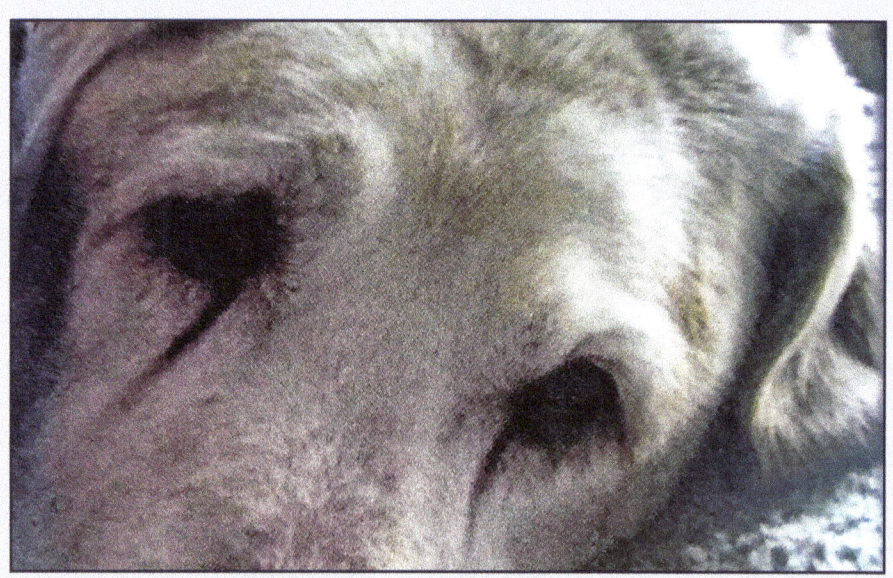

I walked over to the cage where the yellow dog was. At first, I didn't even see her...but she was still there, sitting on the cold, cement floor, way in the back.

She looked sad and scared, and had big wet streaks under her eyes like she had been crying.

No one wanted her because she was so old.

Why wouldn't anyone want this poor dog, even if she *was* old?

I went back home. But I knew I had to do something. Our own dog had died of old age a few months earlier, and we were ready for a new dog. So, I told my husband, Tony, and our five-year-old son, Pablo, that I had found just the right dog for us!

"Trust me," I said.

I was worried, though, that she might not be with us for very long, since she was already older. Pablo thought about it for a few minutes.

"But, Mommy," he said finally, "don't old dogs need homes too?"

That would be the first of many lessons that Bear would teach us.

So, we got in my car and drove right back to the shelter.

Bear Saved!

We walked up to the front desk at the shelter where the man who worked there was sitting. I asked him about the big, yellow dog and a funny look came over his face.

"Uh, wait here just a minute, okay?" he said and ran to the back.

He came back a few minutes later looking relieved and said that we could adopt her. It turns out that they were just about ready to put her to sleep.

Whew! We'd gotten there just in time!

So, we adopted her and took her straight to the veterinarian.

You know what a veterinarian is, don't you? It is a doctor for animals.

Well, first they gave her a good bath … and, boy, did she ever need one!

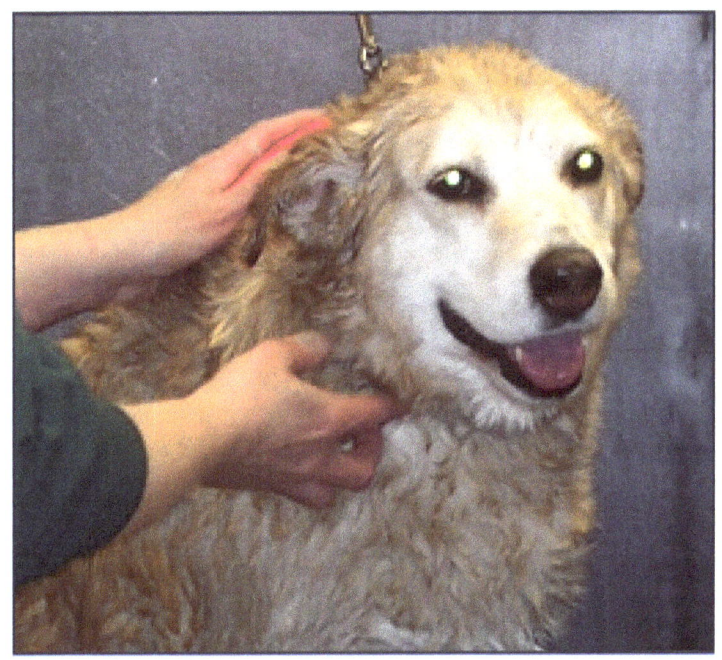

I asked why her eyes were so runny. The assistant looked her over.

"She's healthy." Then she smiled and said, "She's just been crying all week."

I don't know if dogs cry like we do or not, but she sure looked happy now! We took her home and she met Daddy, and they loved each other right away.

Now we had to think of a name. Not just any name. The right name for a girl dog. Hmmmm. Cinnamon? How about Bandit? Freckles? Angel? Or Tubby? (Oh, wait, is that rude?)

Suddenly, Daddy looked at her and said, "Bear!"

Pablo jumped up and ran to the other side of the room.

"Beeaaaar!" he called loudly.

And Bear got up and trotted over to him.

So, Bear it was.

Bear Is Home

When Bear walked into our home, it was like she had been there forever. She got along with everyone!

Pablo and his buddies would race through the house playing knights, yelling and waving their swords high in the air, and she happily chased after them.

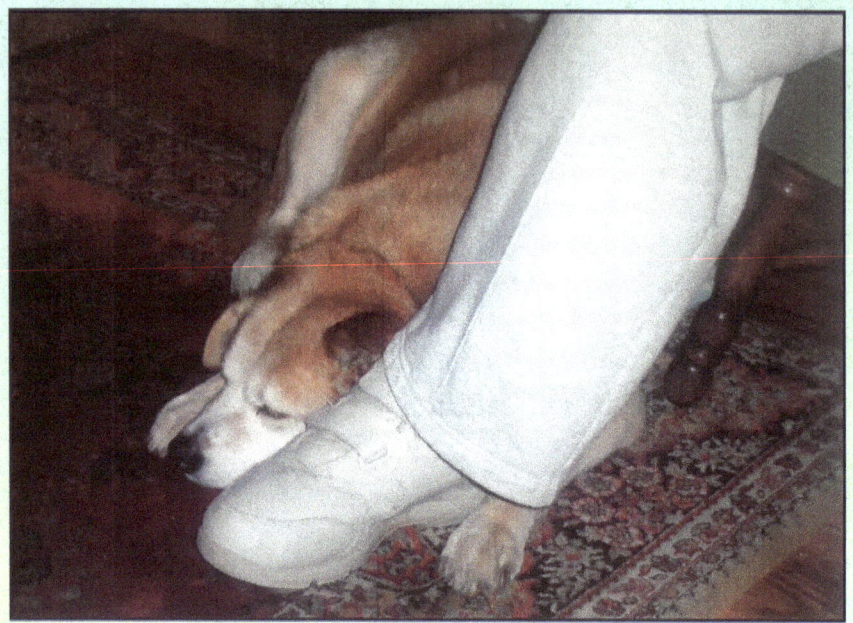

She snuggled up against Daddy when he read the newspaper and stuck to him like glue.

She even tried to jump on our bed once…and since she's pretty big and plump that was a no-no, but it sure made us all laugh!

Pablo really wanted a cat, too. Actually, he wanted a kitten. But Daddy and I told him, "No more pets. Not right now. No way."

Well, one day a big, fluffy, gray cat showed up at our back door and refused to leave. He was skinny and had no collar.

He needed a home.

"Please, Mom, can we keep him?" Pablo begged. "Please?"

We asked around the neighborhood and checked with the animal shelter, but nobody was looking for him or knew anything about him.

"If Bear and he can get along, then you can keep him," I said.

We named the cat Smokey.

Bear was a little bit grumpy about it at first, but Smokey totally ignored her. Bear even tried to chase him a couple of times, but I said, **"No!"** very firmly and in a strict voice, and Bear stopped. (I don't really think Smokey was very worried about it, since he can run a lot faster than Bear can.)

They became buddies and even rubbed noses. Bear and Smokey became part of our family and brought us so much love.

Bear's Favorite Things

As Bear got to know all about us and became part of our family, we learned a few things about her, too.

We learned that she *loves* riding in the car. She went with us pretty much everywhere we went!

She loves cuddling with her toys, especially her favorite stuffed animal, Lambie…

and playing in the snow……

and being brushed (we also learned that Bear sheds a lot!)…

…and that she just loves kids!

Another thing Bear really loves to do is eat. The vet said she was too pudgy. (I think Bear gave her a dirty look when the vet said that.)

So, we put her on a diet, and she lost 8 whole pounds! We were all very proud of her.

But her most favorite thing to do is…

Zzzzzzzzz. . .

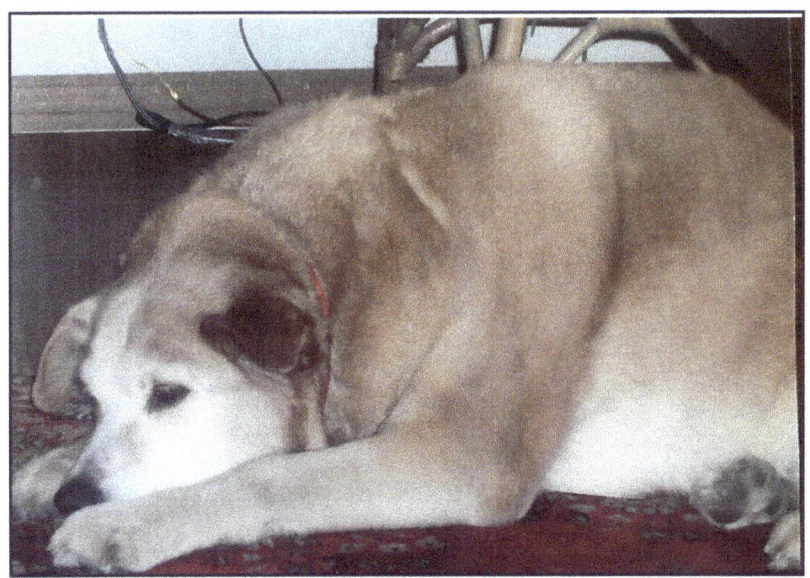

. . .Sleep.

A New Idea

One morning, as Bear was watching TV with us, a lady on the news started talking about a new program they were starting in our city. It was called "Paws to Read," and it was to help children learn to read.

She said that if anyone had a sweet dog who liked kids, to come over to the hospital on Saturday, and they would do a special test to see if the dog would be right for the program.

I looked down at Bear and thought, well, *she* likes kids. Maybe she could help kids learn to read.

So, that Saturday morning, Pablo, Bear, and I drove over to the hospital and walked inside. There was a very serious man holding a clipboard, the lady from the TV news program, and about five other people standing around.

They asked me to fill out a form with all kinds of questions about Bear, like:

1. Has your dog ever bitten anyone?

    No!

2. Does your dog like children?

    Yes!

3. What is your dog's favorite game?

    Being petted and walked.

4. Is your dog afraid of wheelchairs?

    No.

5. What kinds of commands can your dog do?

    Sit, down, stay, come, shake.

6. Is your dog afraid of people wearing hats or beards?

    No.

There. I'd finally filled it all in.

Then we were taken to another room, where Pablo was asked to sit at the far side and to stay out of the way. We were very curious to see what this was going to be all about!

The serious man with the clipboard gave Bear several commands.

He asked me to have her

Sit.

Stay.

Come.

He asked me to walk her around to see how she would react to strangers. The people petted her……and bumped into her……and tried to distract her with toys and treats.

He even brought in another dog to see what she would do, and two of the people there even pretended to yell at each other and have a fight!

Then the man said, "Okay, now I need to see how she'll react to a loud noise," and he suddenly tossed his metal clipboard on the floor!

Did it ever make a racket!

It really startled me, but not Bear. She just ignored it and happily trotted to the other side to investigate.

The man laughed. "Maybe we should check her for vital signs," he joked.

Well, Bear passed the tests and got a diploma of her very own. She even got the highest score possible! That meant that she could work with kids in the reading program and even go into the hospital to visit patients.

We were so happy. Everyone congratulated her, and she got a special treat. We all petted her and told her what a good dog she was.

"Okay," said the serious man. "It's time to get back to work."

"Bye, Bear," they all said as we left. "See you on the job!"

Bear Goes to School

A week later, we got a phone call: Bear had her first assignment!

The local middle school wanted a therapy dog to help out in a reading program for their Lifeskills Special Education students. Wow!

It had been difficult to get a dog at a middle school because some people thought the older kids might be too rowdy or rough. But they thought Bear would be perfect because she was big. Right, I thought. If anyone gives her any nonsense, she can just sit on them!

The day came for Bear's first day at the school. Boy, were we excited!

I helped her into her green vest (which was a little snug over her plump tummy) and her bandana, and put on my own special shirt.

Then, I clipped our official name badge onto her vest.

Bear could hardly wait to get inside that school and meet the kids! She took the steps two at a time (not bad for a ten-year-old), wagging her tail all the way.

The kids were **so** excited to see her!

Bear sat down on her very own pad in the middle of the floor, and all of the kids gathered around in a circle.

Bear happily snuggled her head in the lap of a girl, and lay there looking very content as different students read to her and hugged her. She just loved it.

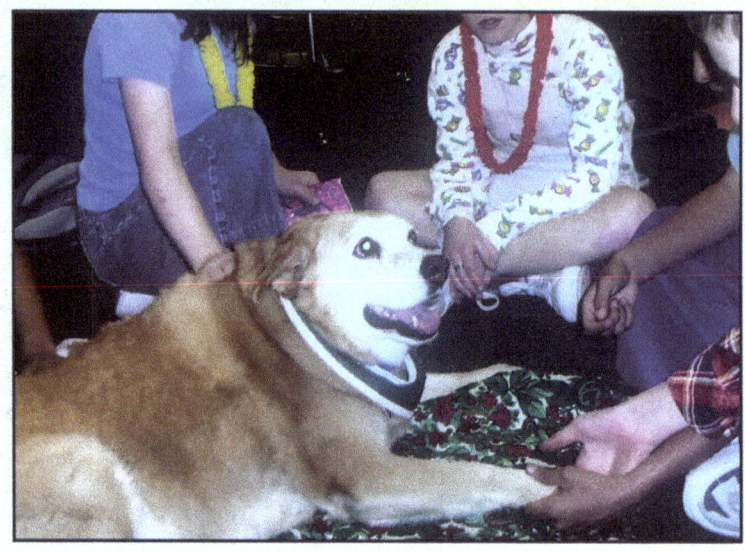

I told them the story of how we had rescued her from the animal shelter, how nobody had wanted her, and how sad and scared she was.

I also told them about all the tests she had to pass in order to come here and be with them.

I showed them our ID badges.

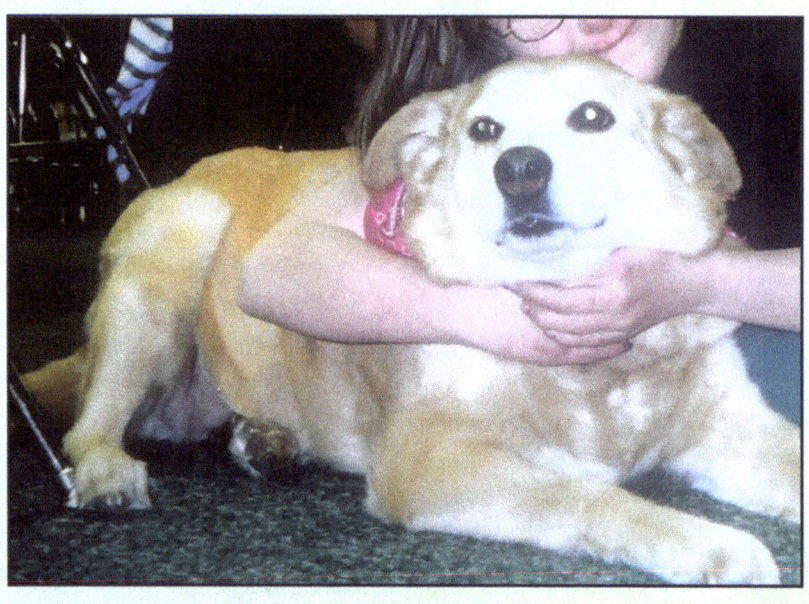

Some of the students pulled out their own student ID cards to show Bear too!

Then she walked around the classroom, getting to know each student, one by one. She sat by their desks or lay on the floor letting each one of them pet her and shake her paw.

Bear's New Friends

We went back week after week, and pretty soon the teacher and I started to see a change in their reading.

"You know," said Ms. Sharp, the teacher, "before Bear came here, some of my students wouldn't read at all. They had trouble reading to an adult, or just didn't want to. Now, all I have to say is 'Bear's coming!' and they run for their books to read to her."

They even researched topics and made special reports to read to Bear, and they talked to her, brushed her, and sometimes got to take her for a little walk around the school.

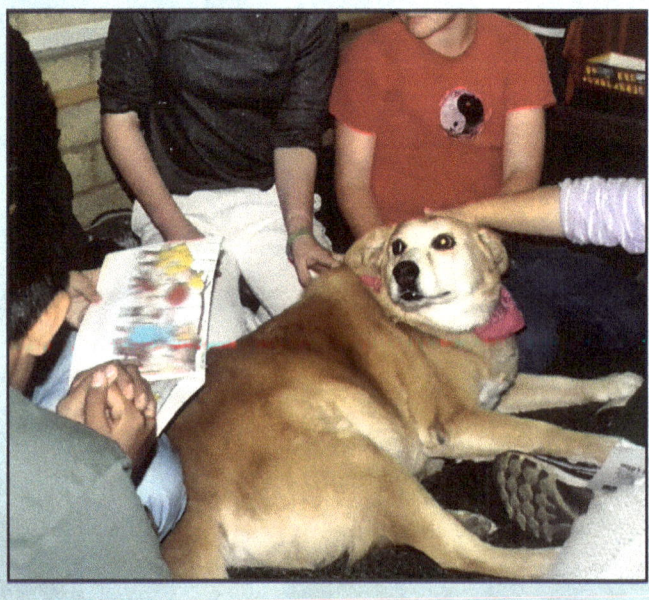

The students read all kinds of interesting stories to Bear.

They read dog stories to her. They read to her about their favorite animals, American Presidents, and national parks.

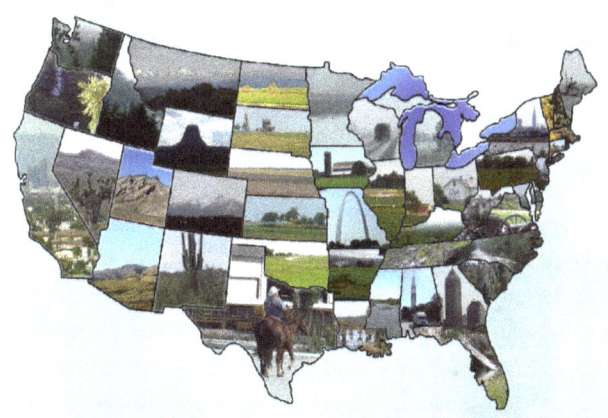

Bear and I learned all about their vacations and trips they'd been on. They talked to her about their feelings and learned that sometimes Bear feels shy, or sad or frustrated, too.

We became a circle of friends with Bear in the middle: learning, growing, sharing and caring.

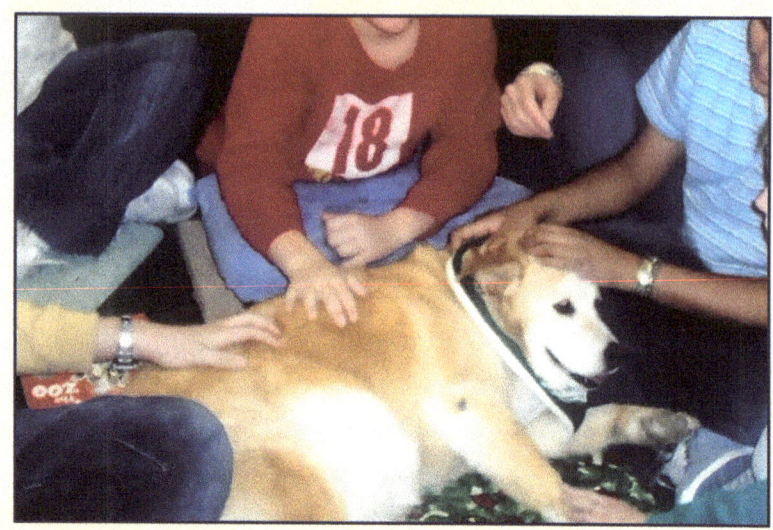

One September, on the first day of school, the principal and her office staff even greeted Bear with applause as she entered the lobby.

Bear also visited with students in other classrooms at the school and got to learn some special things from Native American students, who talked about the sacred mountains and the history of Flagstaff and about the nearby Hopi and Navajo Nations.

Bear loves her job. She loves listening to stories and loves being petted. She doesn't care if their reading isn't perfect yet or if they stumble over words. She doesn't care if they have problems walking or talking or use a wheelchair. She doesn't care if they have light or dark skin, if they speak another language, pray differently, or come from another country. She loves them for who they are, and they love her in return.

They are all her best friends.

One student said, "Bear is very patient when we read. And she's very fuzzy." And they all say, "I love you, Bear."

Once, we all went to the winter Special Olympics at the ski area just outside of Flagstaff on the way to the Grand Canyon. Some of Bear's students were in the competition. We all cheered loudly as "Bear's kids" proudly crossed the finish line in the snowshoe races!

Pablo sometimes came along with Bear and me to special events also. He was very proud of Bear helping these kids learn to read. He read to Bear at home too.

Holidays

One day, we got another call. It was from the lady at the Paws to Read Program.

"Do you have any photographs of Bear?" she asked. "We're going to make a calendar to help raise money for the reading program, and we'd like to put pictures of the dogs in it."

So, I put Bear in the car and drove her to one of my favorite spots, a very pretty meadow with the San Francisco Peaks in the background.

"Stay, Bear," I said. "Say cheese!"

Bear gave me a big smile, and I took a perfect picture of her and sent it in.

In December, Bear and I were invited to the classroom's Christmas party, and it was so much fun. Bear was very excited!

"It's Bear!" the students all cried out, when she came trotting into the room.

A beautiful Christmas tree, with decorations made by the students, stood in the middle of the classroom. There were several gifts underneath.

"There's something for you here, Bear," said one of the students. She sat down on the floor with Bear and opened the gift.

A green tennis ball!

Bear with Lifeskills teacher, Carol Sharp

Then, Ms. Sharp reached under the tree for another gift.

"This one is really special," she said.

Bear sniffed the package and looked excited. What could it be?

Ms. Sharp opened it. Bear's ears perked up and her tail waggled. It was the most beautiful gift a dog could imagine.

A metal tin filled with doggie treats…and on the lid was a photograph of Bear with all the kids!

Then, we all had a visit from Santa, and it was time to go home.

Cover Girl

A while later, I got a message to stop by the Paws to Read office: "We've got something for you and Bear."

We went over and do you know what they gave us? The new Caring Canines Calendar. And guess who was on the cover?

Bear!

Our big, old, pudgy, yellow mutt was a cover girl!

It was so beautiful we just couldn't believe it.

Every one of the students in Bear's class got their very own calendar as a Christmas present, and Bear "autographed" each one with a paw print.

We were invited to a fancy hotel to tell the newspapers about it, and Bear posed with the other dogs next to a big stack of the calendars.

The local TV news even came to the school one day with a reporter who did a special "interview" with Bear and the students.

The kids were so proud to have "their" dog at school. We watched her on that night's evening news!

The month of March brought another reason to celebrate: it was the anniversary of when we'd adopted Bear from the shelter!

The students worked for weeks on their presents for Bear, and even the school principal showed up for the party! When Bear and I walked in, the class was playing the song, "Who Let the Dogs Out" on their CD player and everyone was so happy.

The kids practiced very hard so they could sing to Bear!

There was dancing, home-baked cupcakes with little bears on top, and lots of laughing and fun.

Bear gave every student a birthday gift bag to take home with tooters, dog stickers, pencils, plastic Hawaiian leis, and bouncy balls.

Wow. It was the best birthday she'd ever had!

The end of the school year rolled around, and we got another invitation, this time, to the June class picnic.

We met at a ranch and ate hot dogs and hamburgers. (I think they fed Bear about three of them, and she found some more under the table.)

We had a water balloon fight, and played, and played, and played…all day long. It was a blast! Then it was time to relax, and Bear enjoyed just hanging out with the kids.

During the summer, Bear went to the library to help with their reading program and met some really nice kids there too.

Then, Ms. Sharp and Bear's students had a great idea: they nominated Bear for an award for being such a great therapy dog!

And guess what? She was given a special medal to wear on her collar with the words, "Beyond Limits—Honorable Mention" on it.

Whew! It's been a busy and very happy time for Bear. She's pretty proud of what she's done, and we are, too. Bear was so happy with her classroom buddies.

And you know what? We would have loved her just as much whether or not she had ever been part of the reading program. She brought us so much joy.

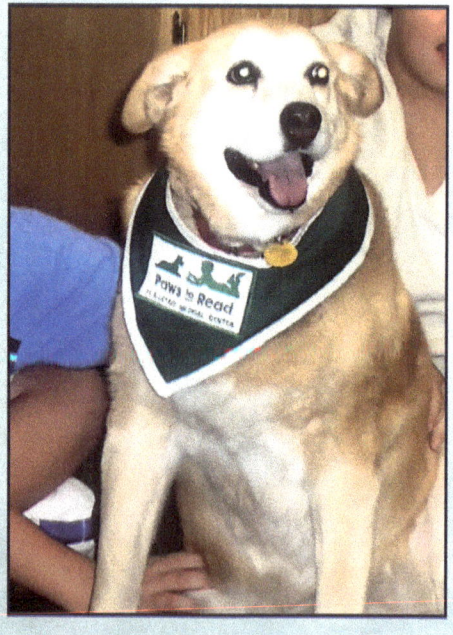

We may have given her a home, but she opened our hearts.

Not bad for a big, old, yellow dog nobody wanted, huh?

But, you know, even with all of this attention, there's one thing that Bear still likes best of all…

Zzzzzzzzzzzzzzz

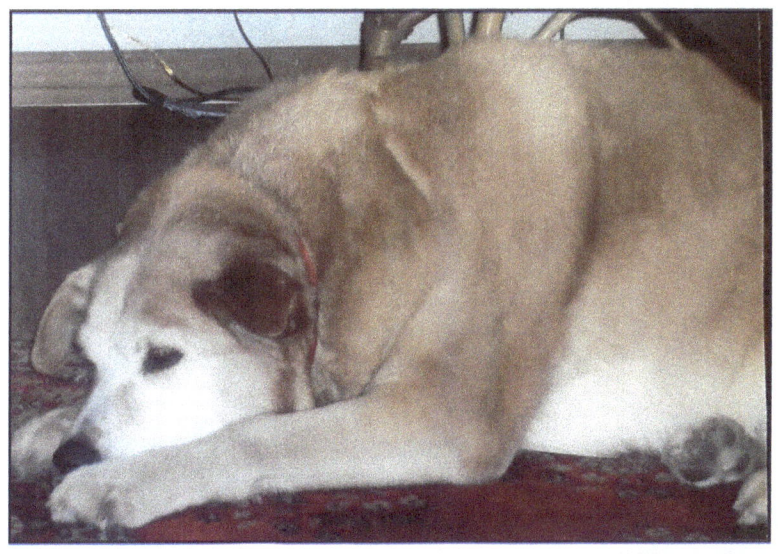

…and, of course, being read to by us and all her friends.

The End

Epilogue

Bear and her family moved from Flagstaff, Arizona to Washington State, where Bear enjoyed her retirement in a big grassy yard with chickens and horses and even a mule right next door. Susanne and Bear continued a lively pen pal correspondence with the students.

Bear passed away at home of old age at the estimated age of fourteen, and her ashes were scattered under her favorite, old apple tree in the back yard where she loved to lie in the shade on hot summer days.

Bear in the Classroom

*Ilona Anderson,
former Principal, Flagstaff Middle School*

When I was principal of Flagstaff Middle School, I was asked if I would be interested in a program called "Caring Canines." After talking with the teacher in the Lifeskills program for students with disabilities, it was decided that Bear would become part of their reading instruction. The students in this program were children of middle school age with Down Syndrome, children with autism, and children with other intellectual or physical disabilities. So, Bear became an integral figure in the teaching of reading to the children.

Susanne would bring Bear, and Bear would sit in the middle of a circle surrounded by the children. Each child would read from his/her book to Bear, while Bear sat ever so patiently. Some of these children had never been able to read before, but because of Bear, they started learning to read. It was Bear who became their inspiration. The children and Bear crossed over the line that sometimes separates animals from humans. Together they entered a space where there was no difference. The children were sure that Bear understood their stories, and Bear was sure that she was one of them.

Without her presence, I know that many of those children would not have learned to read and progress in their reading. More importantly, they grew in their ability to love and care for each other and for Bear. And so, the image in my mind that will remain with me forever is Bear sitting in the circle of love with the children, gently wagging her tail and listening to the children read to her with love in their voices. She touched the lives of every child in that classroom.

About the Author

"My volunteer work with Bear is one of the best, most rewarding things I've ever done. I will always be grateful for the deep friendships and for this unique opportunity to be of service to others."

Susanne Severeid is an award-winning author of numerous books, articles, essays, and poems and has an extensive performing arts background, including hosting an EMMY Award-winning PBS-TV documentary. *Bear: A True Story* is her second children's book.

www.susannesevereid.com

Susanne Severeid with Bear

www.ingramcontent.com/pod-product-compliance
Lightning Source LLC
Chambersburg PA
CBHW061147010526
44118CB00026B/2897